Conte...

Meet the team...

HI, I'M SAL

I love finding out about the past, all the things that happened to get us to now – just amazing!

TURN TO PAGE 6 FOR A BRIEF HISTORY OF THE LAST 250 MILLION YEARS!

HEY, I'M WILL

My mum says I'm a dreamer but I reckon I just like using my imagination. Add a few details to a story, paint with every colour – it makes things so much more interesting!

READ SOME OF THE STORIES TOLD ABOUT THE GIANT'S CAUSEWAY ON PAGE 18.

Get involved

There are lots of things to do, from solving puzzles, making your own boat, to going on a seaside safari!

Get creative

The Giant's Causeway has been inspiring artists and writers for hundreds of years. Is the world ready for your masterpiece?

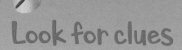
Look for clues

The Giant's Causeway lives up to its name – it's MASSIVE. But don't forget it's the little details that make up the big picture.

AND I'M CRAIG

I love wildlife and the life round here is pretty wild! Birds flying, seals swimming and who knows what's lurking in the rock pools.

FIND OUT MORE ABOUT THE GIANT'S CAUSEWAY'S WILDLIFE ON PAGES 24–27.

Frank facts

Frank the Fulmar will be popping up here and there, giving us his bird's-eye view of the Causeway. Fulmars are a common sight around here but they're a bird you don't want to get too close to. If they feel threatened, they bring up an oily, smelly substance from their stomachs and spit it at their would-be attackers! The Vikings certainly knew about this: the word 'fulmar' is from their language and translates as 'foul gull'!

How on Earth?

The 40,000 pillars of the Giant's Causeway add up to one big puzzle!

The Giant's Causeway is one of the world's most famous collections of rocks. It's made of around 40,000 pillars jam-packed together and stretching out into the sea like a massive, prehistoric pavement. It's been around for millions of years, but only studied by scientists for around 200 years. Not surprisingly, all sorts of stories have been told – some science, some fiction – to explain this wonder of nature.

SO MANY QUESTIONS!

There's a lot to get your head around at the Giant's Causeway. The scenery is breath-taking (literally if the wind's blowing in the right direction!) It can also leave you puzzling. What on Earth…? How on Earth…? When and, for that matter, why on Earth…? All fair questions, deserving of answers. Would it help if I told you …

…THE WORLD'S AN ONION?

Or maybe an enormous scotch egg, one with a diameter of 12,750 km! What we're trying to say here is that underneath the crust of the Earth that you and I walk on every day there are layers – layers of rock that get hotter and runnier the closer to the centre of the Earth you get.

The crust: There are two types – continental crust, which carries land, and oceanic crust, which carries water.

The mantle: The thickest section of the Earth – approximately 2,900 km of it – made of half-melted rock called magma. It's hard at the top but melts the lower down you go.

The outer core: Made of liquid metal – iron and nickel.

The inner core: The centre and hottest part of the Earth. It is solid, also made of iron and nickel, and has temperatures of up

EARTH-SHATTERING STUFF!

The Giant's Causeway may look like a load of cold, hard rock now, but what you're seeing was once super-hot lava that leaked out of the mantle when cracks appeared in the crust. You see, the crust's not in one piece but made of tectonic plates. Imagine these plates sliding, ever so slowly, over the oozy magma below. That's what they've been doing for billions of years, and they're still moving.

Around 250 million years ago, the plates were squashed together, forming a super continent called Pangaea (*pangaea* is ancient Greek for 'all earth'). Then the plates moved again, letting oceans rush in and lava bubble up. The big break up that created the Atlantic Ocean and also the Giant's Causeway happened around 60 million years ago.

With tectonic plates still on the move, it's estimated that the Atlantic Ocean is widening at roughly three centimetres every year — the same rate as your fingernails grow!

Past, present & future worlds

Here you can see how the world looked before and after Pangaea. Remember we said that the plates that make up the Earth's crust are still moving? Some people think that way in the distant future the Earth's plates will come together again to form a new super continent. How do you think the Earth will look in another 250 million years? What do you think that super continent would be called?

250 million years ago

145 million years ago

65 million years ago

The world today

250 million years in the future

The big picture

Ready? This is going to cover a lot of ground! We don't know for sure whether dinosaurs still roamed the Earth when the events that led to the Causeway began, but there's only a few million years in it!

250 million years ago

All the Earth's land is clumped together in one massive super continent called 'Pangaea'.

This skull is from an amphibian that lived about 250 million years ago.

Megalosaurus lived 166 million years ago in what is now southern England. Scientists think that megalosaurus may have been covered in fine feathers, particularly along its back and belly.

200—145 million years ago

The Jurassic period, or 'The Age of Reptiles'.

80 million years ago

Ireland is covered in a warm shallow sea, full of single-celled sea creatures. The skeletons of these creatures, billions and billions of them, settle to the sea floor and turn into a mineral called limestone or chalk. Chalk is the foundation of the Causeway landscape.

You can find fossils along the Antrim coastline that date from the Jurassic period. Whitepark Bay, a 10-minute drive from the Causeway, is full of beautiful examples. Why not start your fossil hunt there? This beauty, called a paltechioceras, was found there—it's around 190 million years old!

65 million years ago

Volcanic eruptions all over the world chuck massive amounts of earth into the atmosphere changing the climate. Plants don't grow, so the herbivorous (veggie) dinos die out and the meat-eaters eventually starve. And if things weren't bad enough, a huge asteroid strikes the Earth near Mexico and finishes them off.

A dinosaur's-eye view of the asteroid strike.

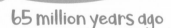

2.6 million — 11,500 years ago

The Earth cools down. Over this time, there are 20 separate cold episodes (ice ages). Very roughly, there was an ice age every 100,000 years or so.

65 — 60 million years ago

By now Ireland has emerged from the sea and vegetation covers its chalky soils. But this peaceful scene is shattered by cracks opening up in the ground and lava flowing out over the land. Lava cools and solidifies. This happens many times during this period of intense volcanic activity: leak, flow, cool, repeat.

2 million years ago

Distant ancestors of humans evolve in East Africa, descended from animals called 'southern apes'.

Does this remind you of anyone you know? This is *Australopithecus africanus*, or the 'southern ape', and she's related to every one of us!

This gigantic deer, *Megaloceros giganteus*, used to roam in Ireland during the last ice age, around 11,500 years ago.

70,000 years ago

Out of six species of humans, *Homo sapiens* (our relations) come out on top. Go us!

The present day

Modern *Homo sapiens* (that's you and me and everyone we know) come to the Giant's Causeway to wonder at the millions and millions and millions of years of earth-shattering history that has gone on right here!

25,000 years ago

Ice sheets cover this part of the world. As they move over the surface of the Earth, they carve out valleys and reveal formations such as the Giant's Causeway.

Looking around today all you see are craggy cliff-faces, crazy paving and crashing waves. It's hard to imagine this place looking any other way, but it has looked very, very different over its long history. For starters, try to imagine it as a deep river valley with a tropical climate and dinosaurs! And then try to imagine the Earth's plates moving under the dinos, sliding apart and letting lava flood out. No wonder they didn't hang around!

COOL SHAPES

Around 60 million years ago the river valley started filling up with lava, lava that has a temperature of between 700 and 1,200°C! (A hot cuppa is about 70°C!) When it came into contact with the air, the surface of the lava quickly cooled, forming a crust. This crust acted like a blanket, stopping the lava below from cooling so quickly, and this slow cooling is what caused the shapes you see today. Because the rock cooled slowly and evenly, it was able to make best use of the space. Think of a honeycomb, another natural structure, which uses five- and six-sided shapes to cram in as much material as possible while keeping the whole thing strong. Another name for the middle part of the Causeway is the Honeycomb Causeway.

The hexagon is a good, strong shape that crops up elsewhere in nature – here in a honeycomb!

SCHOOL OF ROCK

The Giant's Causeway was the result of not just one lava flow but of many that happened over many millions of years. That's a lot of cooled lava – which we call basalt by the way – and it's not just the Giant's Causeway that's made of basalt, but most of County Antrim is made of the stuff. In fact, there were so many lava flows that in places the basalt is over 1,000 metres thick!

All this happened over a huge amount of time and there was a period of about two million years when there were no lava flows. The climate of the time was warm and wet, and it weathered the basalt, creating deep red soil. This is called laterite and you can see layers of it in the cliffs, sandwiched between the dark basalt, showing the break between flows.

BRRRRRR!!!!!

Millions of years after all this intense volcanic activity, the climate was very different. It had cooled dramatically and there were times when much of the Earth's surface was covered in ice. Very roughly, there was an ice age every 100,000 years or so. When people talk about the Ice Age today, if they don't mean the movie, they're generally referring to the most recent one, which was at its iciest about 21,000 years ago and finally thawed out about 11,000 years ago.

THE BIG THAW

All that ice over all those ice ages froze and expanded, melted and shrank, moving out from the poles over the surface of the Earth and carving away the land beneath. This happened at the Giant's Causeway, the earth being scraped away to reveal the pillars of basalt in that ancient river valley. Things warmed up some more, sea levels rose and waves started to wear away the rock.

And there you have it – how to make a Giant's Causeway in 60 and a bit million years!

From lava flows fast-forward a few million years and it was a very different scene! But when the ice started to melt it revealed interesting things beneath!

Anyone order a causeway?

Here's our very brief illustrated history of the Giant's Causeway. Can you match the events with the captions that describe them?

1. Once upon a time, over 60 million years ago, there was a river running through a valley that was covered with plants and trees.

2. Around 60 million years ago, cracks open up in the Earth's crust and out oozes lava. This happens not just once, but lots of times, over time filling up the river valley.

3. The lava in the river valley cools, solidifies and turns into rock, quickly at the top and slowly at the bottom. The slowly cooling lava cracks in even patterns.

4. Things get really chilly. Lots of the Earth's surface is covered in massive, slow-moving glaciers that scrape away at the top layers of rock.

5. Things start to warm up again, the ice melts, the sea levels rise and waves wear away at the rock. When the sea levels drop again, the Causeway is revealed in all its glory!

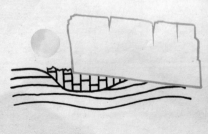

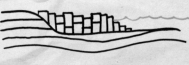

That's not the story I heard!

Massive movements in the Earth's crust, fiery fields of lava, ice ages and glaciers carving their way over the Earth over millions of years.... That's what the scientists would have us believe, but if you've heard of the Giant's Causeway it's likely you've heard of the giant after whom it's named – Finn McCool.

A TALL TALE?

Finn McCool was a giant who, for the most part, lived a quiet life with his wife and baby son here on the Northern Irish coast. But there were rivals, other giants, and there was one in particular Finn didn't much like the look of. You know the sort of thing – big warty nose, one massive eyebrow, knuckles that grazed the floor. This was his Scottish neighbour, Benandonner, and Finn decided to challenge him to do battle.

But as Benandonner lived all the way over in Scotland, Finn had to build a causeway across the sea to reach him – it's a well-known fact that giants hate getting their feet wet! So that's what he did but once Finn's rocky road had reached Scotland, he got a closer look at Benandonner and realised that he was much bigger, uglier and stronger than he'd looked from across the water! Finn decided he didn't want to fight Benandonner after all and ran back home as fast as he could – so fast that he lost a boot! – but not before Benandonner had spotted him and began chasing after him.

Finn got home, found his wife Oonagh and explained the terrible mistake he had made. Oonagh, being the cleverer one, had the idea of dressing Finn up as a baby and putting him into their son Oisín's cot.

Just then there was a loud banging at the door – Benandonner! 'Where's Finn?' he demanded, 'I want to fight him!' 'Calm down!' said Oonagh, 'Finn's out looking after his cows. Why don't you come and wait for him and I'll make you a cup of tea?' So Benandonner had his cup of tea but grew impatient. 'Where's Finn?' he roared. Oonagh explained again, 'He's out herding the cows but while you're here why don't you say hello to our son Oisín?'

When Benandonner saw the MASSIVE baby in the cot he got scared. He thought, if that's the size of the baby, how big is the daddy?! Benandonner immediately ran out of the house and home across the Causeway, tearing it up behind him to way to make sure the baby's dad couldn't follow him.

Sounds like a fairy tale? Well, there's evidence to prove that Finn really built his bridge all the way to Scotland. You can see the other end of Finn's Causeway across the water on the Scottish island of Staffa (or you can just look on page 12).

 **Read all about it!**

Imagine the giants had met and done battle. Who do you think would have won? How would you have reported it? Include eye-witness accounts and, of course, a picture!

THE
Causeway Chronicle

Max 11°C / Min 5°C   Sunday 1 April 2018 / no. 7194   Since 1688

GIANTS GO TO WAR!

The warrior Finn McCool appears in many myths. He was famously fair-haired—his Irish name *Fionn* means 'fair'. He was the leader of the Fianna, a band of warriors. Finn loved animals, especially his dog, who was an Irish wolfhound called Bran.

Flows around the world

The Giant's Causeway is amazing but not unique. Here are some other famous formations, some many, many miles away but all formed as a result of the same earth-shattering movement of plates that caused the North Atlantic Ocean to open up.

Where in the world?

Can you label the map to match up with the numbered descriptions of these formations? ✗ marks the spot of our Causeway!

ARCTIC OCEAN

ARCTIC CIRCLE

ATLANTIC OCEAN

1 Doon Point, Rathlin Island, Northern Ireland

A close relation of the Giant's Causeway just across the water. These columns are thought to be even older than the Causeway.

PACIFIC OCEAN

2 Fingal's Cave, Island of Staffa, Scotland

Further away, across the North Channel (the bit that connects the Irish Sea with the Atlantic Ocean), is Fingal's Cave. Fingal is the Scottish version of the Causeway giant – Finn McCool. Proof of the legendary bridge that Finn built to do battle with Benandonner?

4 Svartifoss, Iceland

A hard name to say without giggling, Svartifoss translates from the Icelandic as 'The Black Falls'. It's one of many such formations on this icy island just outside the Arctic Circle.

EQUATOR

3 The Faroe Islands

You'll find these halfway between Iceland and Norway, although they actually belong to Denmark! There are 18 rocky, volcanic islands that formed after a series of lava flows, just like those at the Causeway but even more so – these built up to a depth of nearly 3,000 metres!

5 Disko Island, Greenland

Does this sound like the coolest place or what?! Well inside the Arctic Circle, it's cooler than cool and it's the most northerly point of that break in the tectonic plates that created the Atlantic Ocean.

6 Rocha dos Bordões, Flores Island, Azores

Sitting in the middle of the Atlantic Ocean at a point where not two but three tectonic plates meet, the islands of the Azores formed from lava bubbling up between these cracks in the crust. *Rocha dos Bordões* is Spanish for 'Walking Stick Cliff'. Sounds like one for the oldies but these are babies compared to the rest – they appeared just seven million years ago!

7 Los Organos, La Gomera, Canary Islands

Lying off the west coast of Africa and named after the columns you'd find in church organs, these basalt pillars are nearly 800 metres tall! Finn McCool also played the organ, although his is a tiddler by comparison, just 12 metres tall.

INDIAN OCEAN

PACIFIC OCEAN

The 'pipes' of the Giant's Organ at the Causeway are tall but nothing compared to Los Organos!

SOUTHERN OCEAN

Discovery!

Obviously the locals knew about the Giant's Causeway since forever – it's pretty hard not to notice! But it took a while for the rest of the world to find out about this place and of course they were amazed. Like a lot of people who come to see the Causeway today, they couldn't quite believe this wasn't man-made.

THE FIRST TOURIST

The first person to write about the Giant's Causeway was a man called Robert Redding. That was in 1688. He'd clearly seen nothing like this before! He wrote: "there are a vast quantity of Hexagonall Pillars of stone about 8 Inches side…. These Columns are so regularly ranged and fitted one to the other that it seems rather the work of art than nature."

A WORK OF ART

Word spread of this wonder of nature and along with scientists seeking answers came artists seeking inspiration. Susanna Drury came from Dublin to paint the scene and her watercolours are the first accurate views we have of the Causeway. As well as details of the columns, she included people in her paintings wearing the fashions of the day, which was around 1740. You can see ladies in their best dresses with huge skirts – not the best thing to wear in the winds that usually whip around the Causeway!

Susanna entered her paintings into a competition held by the Dublin Society and won first prize! Her paintings were made into engravings that got sent all over the world. This made the Causeway famous and brought many, many tourists eager to see this amazing sight for themselves.

One of Susanna Drury's award-winning watercolours.

Susanna's paintings went down so well with the Dublin Society that she won prize money of £25!

Create your own Causeway

Susanna Drury's paintings helped bring the Giant's Causeway to the world's attention and even won her a prize! Can you create your own work of art to rival hers? (Sorry, we're not offering any prizes here!)

Rocks in the post

Does your mum or dad work from home? Well so did the scientist famous for making the Causeway, er, famous!

POOR POSTMAN!

Sir Thomas Molyneux was the first person to seriously study the Giant's Causeway and for that his name's known to this day. But amazingly, he never saw the Causeway for himself!
He lived in Dublin about 150 miles away, a tricky but not impossible journey in those days, but he preferred to stay at home in his study. There he'd read his weighty, leather-bound books and write letters. To help him learn about the Causeway he had someone local send him descriptions and even break off bits of rock and post them to him. Can you imagine receiving a whole load of rocks in the mail?!

DETAILED DRAWINGS

Sir Thomas Molyneux was good at getting other people to do things for him. He paid an artist called Edwin Sandys to produce some drawings of the rocks at the Giant's Causeway. These beautiful and detailed drawings (here and on the next page) showed a special feature of the columns – that they were made of sections that stacked up and fitted together in a particular way. The top of one section curves in like a bowl and the section above it bulges at the bottom, so they fit together really snugly. This is called a ball and socket joint, the sort of joint you have in your body, like where your arm slots into your shoulder.

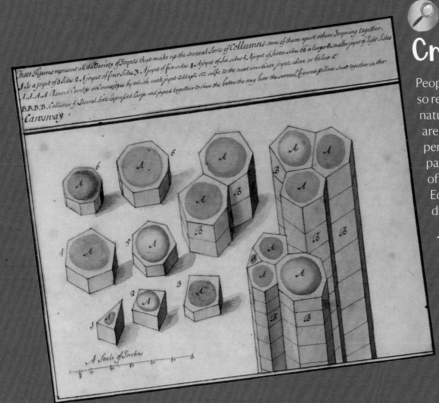

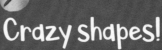

Crazy shapes!

People have struggled to believe that something so regular and geometric could have happened naturally. But geometry and mathematical patterns are actually found throughout nature – think of the perfect symmetry of a snowflake, or the repeated patterns in a peacock's tail. Here's the geometry of the Giant's Causeway. In this detail from Edwin Sandys' drawing you can see all the different shapes that the columns come in.

Three-sided
(triangular)

Four-sided
(quadrilateral)

Five-sided
(pentagonal)

Six-sided
(hexagonal)

Seven-sided
(heptagonal)

Eight-sided
(octagonal)

Hexagon wordsearch

Do you see how in Edwin Sandys' drawing that some columns of the Giant's Causeway are lots of hexagons locked into a pattern like a honeycomb? Here we've locked a whole load of words into our very own honeycomb. There are 12 to find and, to make things a bit trickier, they don't all run in straight lines. We've found the first one to get you started.

BALL
SOCKET
STUDY
MOLYNEUX
PILLAR
POST
DUBLIN
BASALT
ROCK
SANDYS
JOINT
SCIENTIST

Masses of Myths

The Irish are some of the best storytellers around, and something like the Giant's Causeway inspires all sorts of stories. You've heard one version of what happened here, but there are plenty more. Which would you believe?

Cinderella had her glass slipper, Finn had this ugly old boot!

A TRAGIC LOVE STORY?

Some soppy folk reckon Finn built the Causeway to reach a fair Scottish maiden he'd fallen in love with. But his Granny didn't think much of his running off with this girl, so after Finn had spent the day busily building, she used her witchly powers to stir up the sea and destroy what he'd done. The next day he'd start building over, and Granny did it again. This happened time and time again until, one day, Finn keeled over dead from exhaustion. Granny clambered up a hill to see how Finn was getting on and, when she saw what she'd done, she was so horrified she turned to stone. If you look, you'll see her standing there still to this day.

Can you see Granny, frozen in horror staring out to sea?

Where's the evidence?

Myths they may be, but there are some clues lying about that back up parts of the story. See this massive stone polished smooth by the sea? Well, what if we told you it wasn't a stone but the left boot of a giant in a big hurry? In our original story Finn ran as fast as he could away from bug-ugly Benandonner, so quickly that his boot came off and he didn't stop to pick it up. The laces came loose too and got washed up further along the coast where they were used to build the rope bridge at Carrick-a-Rede. People have studied the evidence and worked out with this size of boot – 93½ to be precise – Finn must have been over 16 metres tall!

CAMEL CABS

One story goes that Finn found himself far from home and needed to get back in a hurry. So what did he do? He hailed a giant galloping camel of course! Once he got home, Finn had clearly taken a liking to his camel and decided to keep him. He called him Humphrey and he's still here!

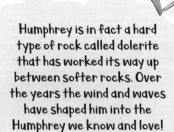

Humphrey is in fact a hard type of rock called dolerite that has worked its way up between softer rocks. Over the years the wind and waves have shaped him into the Humphrey we know and love!

Handily, Finn's laces were long enough to build this rope bridge eight miles along the coast.

Humphrey resting after giving Finn a back-breaking lift home!

✋ Another fishy tale

There's another story about Finn that explains how he got to be so clever and could keep one step ahead of his opponents. (Hang on, wasn't that his wife?)

When he was young, Finn studied under a druid called Finnéces. After seven years trying to catch the Salmon of Knowledge, Finnéces finally caught it and told his pupil to cook it for him. While cooking the salmon, Finn burned his thumb and, without thinking, stuck it in his mouth. After that he did a whole lot more thinking – he'd just gained all the knowledge in the world! Not surprisingly, Finnéces was not a happy chappie. The part of the story we know to be true is that eating salmon boosts your brainpower. And we know there are plenty of salmon around here – salmon fishing used to be a major industry on this part of the coast. Go see our friends at Carrick-a-Rede and they'll tell you all about it. For now, join the dots for your catch of the day.

Shipwrecked!

Ill-tempered giants aren't the only ones to have declared war round here. Back in the summer of 1588 the English and Spanish weren't getting on at all well. The Spanish sent their Armada – a fleet of 130 ships – to invade, but the English navy fought them off using fireships and forced the Spanish to flee. But that was just the start of their problems…

OUT OF THE FRYING PAN…

Into the fire? Well, actually no, into something much wetter. The Spanish had to get out of hostile English waters, so the surviving ships headed up to and around Scotland, where they got caught up in the storms of the North Atlantic. One of these ships, *La Girona*, met her end on 26 October 1588 after she hit the rocks of Lacada Point, a little way along the coast from the Causeway. Of the 1,300 men on board – many more than there would normally be as they'd picked up sailors from other shipwrecks – just nine survived. After being sheltered for a while in the village of Dunluce, they were taken to safety in Scotland.

This is what *La Girona* would have looked like before being smashed to pieces on rocks near the Causeway!

A LONG, WATERY WAIT

Nearly 400 years passed. The details of what had happened to *La Girona* had become as murky as the waters in which she lay. Some of the locals actually made up stories about what had happened and where *La Girona* had gone down to throw treasure-hunters off the scent. But then in 1967, a Belgian diver and historian called Robert Sténuit pieced together the clues and found her and all her treasure! In total, over many dives, they spent more than 6,000 hours recovering 12,000 items, including gold, jewellery and cannons.

Clues in the name?

You don't have to speak Spanish to think there might have been a clue to *La Girona's* watery whereabouts. The name of the bay where it was eventually found? Port na Spaniagh! Err, hello-o! Lacada Point is a funny one as, although it sounds Spanish, it actually comes from the Gaelic *Leac Fhada*, meaning 'long flagstone'.

FINDERS KEEPERS?

With such an important and valuable discovery, obviously the question of who should keep the treasure came up. Spain claimed it belonged to them, while others argued that it should stay in Northern Ireland. In the end, a court decided that no single owner could be found, so the objects would have to be sold. They were valued at £132,000 and Sténuit agreed a deal for the collection to stay in Northern Ireland and in the Ulster Museum, where you can see the Girona gold on display.

This salamander is made with rubies from Burma and gold from South America. At this time Spain ruled over large parts of the world. These creatures were believed to have power over fire, so were carried for good luck by sailors of wooden ships.

The hunt for treasure

La Girona was carrying all sorts of valuables when she sank close to the Causeway. There's a story that James McDonnell of nearby Dunluce Castle took some treasure from the wreckage to make repairs to his castle! But there were still plenty of precious objects on the seabed when the divers made their discovery nearly 400 years later. Can you find some of the things they did?

LEAD   COINS
GOLD   BRASS
SILVER   JEWELLERY
RINGS   CANNON
CHAINS   SALAMANDER
AMULETS   RUBIES

D	F	G	H	M	I	R	I	N	G	S	A	F	G	J	S
A	I	O	N	B	M	U	G	X	V	G	U	Y	I	L	D
B	S	F	B	N	A	B	Q	W	G	H	I	O	R	C	F
N	I	A	R	A	M	I	C	D	E	R	A	H	M	H	G
M	T	J	L	W	G	E	A	F	I	J	W	R	T	A	H
K	E	D	N	A	V	S	I	L	V	E	R	D	O	I	J
A	V	D	R	L	M	A	M	G	C	W	L	M	I	N	K
B	R	A	S	S	T	A	S	G	H	E	A	J	F	S	I
G	E	M	O	Q	H	M	N	A	P	L	E	A	D	A	Y
A	J	S	Q	H	U	O	L	D	R	L	A	F	H	L	T
E	K	N	R	T	N	W	D	T	E	E	D	V	N	F	R
U	S	I	H	N	A	T	G	H	K	R	A	V	M	G	E
D	Y	O	A	V	W	S	R	J	A	Y	P	I	L	J	W
X	G	C	S	E	D	H	I	L	M	K	L	U	A	O	S
A	D	B	N	T	L	M	E	S	T	E	L	U	M	A	T
Y	G	O	L	D	V	B	E	M	G	H	I	E	T	K	L

These gold coins were recovered from the wreck of the *La Girona* and are now in the Ulster Museum in Belfast.

Still telling tales

Millions of people have come to the Giant's Causeway, and they've been coming for hundreds of years! Look at these photos and you'll see faces and fashions from long ago. And for as long as people have been coming, there's been a warm welcome as well as guides eager to tell their tales about the Causeway.

These guides look mostly friendly but competition for business was fierce!

EARNING A LIVING

Way back in 1708, people were already taking guided tours of the Causeway. We know that from an account written by Samuel Molyneux about his visit. (That name sound familiar? He was the nephew of Sir Thomas!) These guides were all local, some started as young as 15 and others were still guiding well into their 80s! They must have thought it easier and safer work than fishing out at sea.

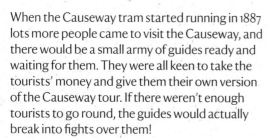

Tourists would sometimes be fought over for their business!

STEADY ON GUIDES!

When the Causeway tram started running in 1887 lots more people came to visit the Causeway, and there would be a small army of guides ready and waiting for them. They were all keen to take the tourists' money and give them their own version of the Causeway tour. If there weren't enough tourists to go round, the guides would actually break into fights over them!

The Causeway tram was super green as it was the world's very first tram powered by hydroelectricity! The water came from the River Bush.

SEEN FROM THE SEA

A boat tour used to be an essential part of any day trip to the Causeway. Up to 20 passengers would be loaded into seven-metre long rowboats and taken all along the coast. They'd even be taken into caves, and in one of them someone would be waiting with a gun that they'd fire off a) to show the visitors how sounds were magnified in the cave and b) to scare the poor tourists half to death! The National Trust took over the Causeway in 1961 and decided not to take visitors out to sea and not to fire guns near them for entertainment!

It doesn't look much safer in the rowboats!

KING OF THE GUIDES

There was one guide who was particularly famous and he was guiding visitors well before the National Trust took over the care of the Causeway and carried on for years after. Alec Martin was 'King of the Causeway' and would entertain visitors with his stories as well as offer them souvenirs he'd made himself!

Row your own boat

Early visitors, the brave ones anyway, took their tours from little rowboats! You can't take a boat tour any more, but you can make your own boat! Here's how…

1 Take a piece of A4 paper and fold it in half like so.

2 Fold it in half again and open it up.

3 Fold the top corners in to the middle crease like this.

4 Hold the bottom of the side facing you and fold up over the triangles.

5 Flip it over and fold down the little triangles poking up over the other side.

6 Then fold the bottom up to cover the folded-down triangles.

7 From this shape open it up in the other direction and flatten.

8 It'll look like this.

9 Now take hold of the point at the bottom and fold it up to the top.

10 Flip it over and fold the other point up.

11 Open it up again and flatten.

12 Gently pull apart from the points at the top and – ta dah! – a rowboat.

Causeway Wildlife

The Causeway is one massive wonder of nature millions of years old. But there are also living wonders of nature creeping, crawling, swimming, fishing and flying all over the place! Some are easier to spot than others, but all these are here if you look hard enough.

FEATHERY FRIENDS

We all know Frank now but there are masses of other bird species that also call the Causeway home, at least for part of the year.

Eider duck

These ducks make their nests in crevices on and around the Causeway. Eiderdown – soft feathers from the mother's breast – is used to line the nests to keep the young nice and cosy. You may have heard the name before, as these feathers are sometimes used to fill quilts and duvets.

Oystercatchers

These prefer to nest in the open, sometimes on the top of the columns themselves! They're easy to spot with their bright red legs and long orange bill, which they use to prise open shellfish.

Razorbill

This stocky black and white bird normally lives out at sea, only coming onto land to breed. If you see them up close there's that distinctive bill of course, but you may notice them fishing off shore, diving into the water when they see an eel or fish. They can even use their wings as paddles to chase their prey underwater!

Even more tourists!

Some birds live here all year, but some come for their annual holidays. Wheatears and grasshopper warblers both travel all the way from Africa to nest at the Causeway.

Grasshopper warbler in mid-warble!

UNDER THE SEA

The sea around the Giant's Causeway is full of watery wildlife, but seals are a favourite with visitors as well as the people lucky enough to work here. We've got both common and grey seals. Greys are actually commoner, and they breed on the rocky coast around the Causeway from September to December. They're wary of humans but can sometimes be spotted playing offshore.

A young grey seal in big brown seaweed, known as kelp.

Basking sharks are the second-largest fish in the world: only the whale shark is bigger.

Seals spend most of their lives in the water. They can even sleep there by doing something called 'bottling'. They get into an upright position with just their heads above water.

If you wanted big, nothing in the waters round here gets bigger than this! Basking sharks can grow up to 8 metres – as long as a house is tall! But if you see the tip of their metre-tall fin sticking out of the water, don't panic and scream 'SHARK!' Basking sharks only feed on plankton, tiny drifting organisms that live in the surface layers of the sea.

Barnacles (the little ones) and limpets (the big ones)

What's washed up?

At low tide rock pools become little aquariums, letting you get up close to various water-loving creatures without you even having to get your feet wet! Just remember, it's always better to look and not touch. Once you've found one of the animals, put a tick beside it.

Periwinkles

Crab

Sea anemone

Dog whelk

Shrimp

Common starfish

Watch your step!

Thousands of basalt pillars making a pavement out to sea. The skies and the seas teeming with life. There's enough here to make your head spin! But that's not even all there is to see – you just need to look a little more closely, and watch where you tread!

WHAT GROWS HERE?

You might think that plants would have a hard time growing at the Giant's Causeway. It's true, a lot of plants would struggle to make a home here among the rocks, being lashed by the wind and the rain. But that just makes the plants that do grow here that much more amazing.

A cheap way of getting the taste of oysters?

Plucky plants

The oysterplant is usually found on the shingle near the sea, and has silvery-green leaves and produces tiny blue flowers in summer. It gets its name because its leaves taste of oysters. Pretty salty then! We don't recommend you trying it for yourself.

Also look out for Scots lovage, which is only found in Northern Ireland and Scotland. Also rare is sea spleenwort, which is a type of fern you'll find growing in crevices in the rocks.

Some plants add a real splash of colour to the Causeway in the summer months, when you'll see clumps of bird's-foot trefoil (yellow), sea campion (white) and sea pinks (you can work out what colour they are!).

The caterpillar of the pygmy sorrel moth feeds inside the leaf of common sorrel found on the slopes here at the Giant's Causeway. It is Britain's smallest moth and really is tiny – just 3 mm from the tip of one wing to the other. The Giant's Causeway is the only place it's been recorded in Northern Ireland.

LIVING ROCKS!

One of the most amazing discoveries at the Causeway was made in a shallow puddle in 2012. It was a colony of stromatolites, which are tiny blue-green bacteria that can photosynthesise like plants. Over thousands of years these build up into a hard rock that continues to grow. This may not sound like much, until you discover that these are one of the earliest life forms on Earth, first appearing three billion years ago, long before the dinosaurs. Adding to the excitement of the discovery is the fact that stromatolites are usually found in salty lakes in warmer countries, for example Australia, Brazil and Mexico, so it was a huge surprise when they were found living in fresh water in Northern Ireland!

These funny-looking lumps of algae have existed on Earth for 3,000,000,000 years!

Who lives where?

Can you match these Causeway residents to their habitats?

1 Basking on a sunny slope

Stonechat

Fox moth caterpillar

2 Perched around patches of scrub

Common lizard

3 Flitting about in grass near the top of the cliffs

5 Skittering on the steep slopes around the Causeway

Ants

Grayling butterfly

4 Crawling around in grassy banks

Farewell from Frank

Well I hope you've been blown away by what you've seen here at the Giant's Causeway, and not just by the wind – it can get pretty wild! What you've seen is so special that it's been declared a World Heritage Site (WHS). This means it gets extra special care and attention, because what's here is so important. Which suits me fine because this is my home!

WHAT'S WHS?

A World Heritage Site is a landmark or area that has been officially recognised by the United Nations Educational, Scientific and Cultural Organization (UNESCO). There are over a thousand of them around the world. There are three types of World Heritage Site – natural, cultural and a mix of the two. The Giant's Causeway made the list in 1986, not only for the amazing beauty of its landscape but also because of what it tells us about Earth's ancient past.

TAKE CARE

I don't need to tell you why it's so important we look after these places. It's pretty obvious to me and I'm a bird! We've only got this one world and the things on it are finite, which means that they'll run out one day, and that day will come sooner if we're not careful. For example, if you humans catch too many fish or pollute the waters and kill them off, then what am I supposed to eat?!

So go and tell all your friends about this amazing place. It might be the first World Heritage Site you've visited, but let's hope you get out there and see some more of the world's amazing wonders.

The world's heritage

The Giant's Causeway is certainly special, but there are plenty of others around the world. See if you can identify these places. You can ask grown-ups for help – after all, they should be interested in this stuff too!

1

2

3

4

5

6

Take our giant quiz!

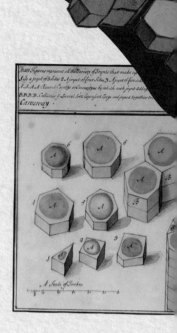

1

All the world's lands were once part of a giant super continent; what was it called?

A Atlantis
B Gaia
C Pangaea
D Frangipane

2

The part of the Earth made of liquid metal is called what?

A The mantle
B The inner core
C The outer core
D Cor, it's hot in here

3

What was the name of the fabled Scottish giant that Finn built his Causeway to meet and fight?

A Benjamin
B Benandjerry
C Benandonner
D Benfogle

4

These are some amazing collections of columns, minus a few letters. Can you fill in the blanks?

D _ _ N P _ I _ T

_ _ _ G A L'S C _ _ E

S _ A R T _ F _ S S

L _ S O R _ _ N _ S

5

The Giant's Causeway and formations like it are all made of a volcanic rock called what?

A Asphalt
B Basalt
C Chalk
D Limestone

6

What was the name of the artist who famously painted the Giant's Causeway picking up a prize in the process?

A Susanna Drew
B Susanna Drury
C Susanna Dreary
D Susanna Dandy

7

Sir Thomas Molyneux was the first person to study the Giant's Causeway in detail, but he never visited it for himself! How did he manage it?

A He visited similar rock formations
B He got someone to send him bits of the Causeway in the mail
C He sent someone to take photos
D He googled it

8

How do we describe the way the sections of columns fit together?

A Ball and chain
B Bat and ball
C Hinge and bracket
D Ball and socket

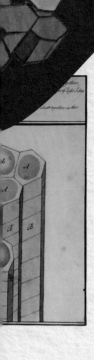

9

The many-sided shapes of the columns at the Causeway are its most famous feature. Can you match up the following?

five-sided	heptagonal
six-sided	pentagonal
seven-sided	octagonal
eight-sided	hexagonal

10

Humphrey the camel is not really a camel at all, but a camel-shaped bit of very hard rock. What is this type of rock called?

A Dolerite
B Laterite
C Ammonite
D Vegemite

11

With size 93½ feet, Finn is thought to have been how tall? Here's a clue: the average man has size 10 feet and is 1.8 metres tall.

A Around 6 metres
B Nearly 10 metres
C Over 16 metres
D Around 60 metres

12

Which country did the sailors on board the galleon *La Girona* come from?

A Mexico
B Scotland
C Spain
D England

13

Here are some birds that you'll find at the Giant's Causeway but we've jumbled them up! Which feathery friends are these?

A BRAZILLOR
B ERSCRATCHYTOE
C DUKE CIDER
D AWEATHER

14

What do basking sharks eat?

A Seals
B Unwary tourists
C Plankton
D Large fish

15

Stromatolites first appeared on Earth three billion years ago! That's a lot of zeros, but just how many?

A 30,000
B 300,000
C 3,000,000
D 3,000,000,000

Answers

Inside front cover

Odd one out!

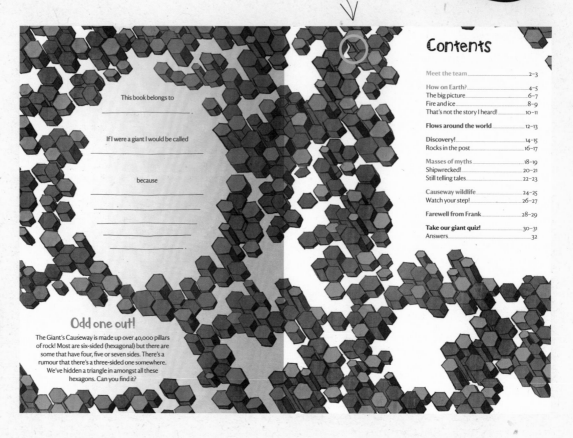

This book belongs to
_____

If I were a giant I would be called
_____

because
_____
_____
_____
_____
_____

Odd one out!

The Giant's Causeway is made up over 40,000 pillars of rock! Most are six-sided (hexagonal) but there are some that have four, five or seven sides. There's a rumour that there's a three-sided one somewhere. We've hidden a triangle in amongst all these hexagons. Can you find it?

Contents

Page 9

Anyone order a causeway?

1 Once upon a time, over 60 million years ago, there was a river running through a valley that was covered with plants and trees.

2 Around 60 million years ago, cracks open up in the Earth's crust and out oozes lava. This happens not just once, but lots of times, over time filling up the river valley.

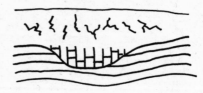

3 The lava in the river valley cools, solidifies and turns into rock, quickly at the top and slowly at the bottom. The slowly cooling lava cracks in even patterns.

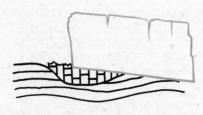

4 Things get really chilly. Lots of the Earth's surface is covered in massive, slow-moving glaciers that scrape away at the top layers of rock.

5 Things start to warm up again, the ice melts, the sea levels rise and waves wear away at the rock. When the sea levels drop again, the Causeway is revealed in all its glory!